© 1992 Benedikt Taschen Verlag GmbH
Hohenzollernring 53, D-5000 Köln 1
© 1990 Claus Wickrath, 10 rue Mallet-Stevens,
F-75016 Paris
Traduction française: Marie-Anne Trémeau-
Böhm, Cologne
Deutsche Übersetzung: Eva Alevisos, Köln
Printed in Germany
ISBN 3-8228-9776-0

CLAUS WICKRATH
flowerskin

Benedikt Taschen

As one who believes that, on balance, Socrates' powers of thought were greater than Newton's, it follows that I offer Claus the highest of accolades when I say that he too has that uncommon characteristic of being *emotionally logical*.

It would be tempting, but untrue, to say that his mind is ruled by his heart and not by his head.

Claus is far too contradictory a person for that.

While he is an inconsummate dreamer, he is also capable of intense concentration and is one of the hardest workers I have ever encountered.

He lives life extravagantly, but this prodigality is of little import to him.

One always has a suspicion that the next time Claus leaves the room, it will be to sneak out and buy himself a horribly overpriced state-of-the-art rucksack and to disappear over the horizon.

There is a naïveté about him but, as with most artists, this lends sophistication to his work.

Claus says yes more often than he should and is forever in the unfortunate position of having taken on more that he should have, yet, unusually, he always finds or makes time for himself, his friends and for his ideas.

These contradictions seem to sit well with Claus.

Contrary to most talented and successful individuals, there is no cloud waiting to darken his mood.

At times it appears as though he actively enjoys the inconsistencies of his world and of his own many-sided character.

Indeed he seems to find succour in them.

Claus is not an artist who suffers. He is a happy one who, if anything, is titillated by his plight.

Perhaps it is his ability to tame the gremlins in his own world that enables him to cut through the dross of professional photography and hang on to his honesty, his purity and his poetry.

Dream on, Claus.

David Colby

Meiner Meinung nach war die Gedankenkraft von Sokrates alles in allem größer als die Newtons – ich spreche also Claus mein höchstes Lob aus, wenn ich sage, daß auch er die ungewöhnliche Eigenschaft besitzt, auf gefühlsmäßige Art logisch zu sein.

Die Versuchung liegt nahe, zu behaupten, daß sein Denken nicht von seinem eigenen Kopf, sondern von seinem Herzen gelenkt wird, aber das ist nicht wahr.

Dafür ist Claus eine viel zu widersprüchliche Person.

Obwohl er sich gern Träumereien hingibt, ist er doch zu starker Konzentration imstande und einer der fleißigsten Menschen, denen ich je begegnet bin.

Er führt ein extravagantes Leben, aber diese Verschwendung bedeutet ihm wenig.

Man hat immer den Verdacht, Claus würde sich das nächste Mal, wenn er den Raum verläßt, davonstehlen, einen grauenhaft überteuerten, ultramodernen Rucksack kaufen und dann hinter dem Horizont verschwinden.

Er hat etwas Naives an sich, wie bei den meisten Künstlern wird seine Arbeit gerade durch diese Naivität so anspruchsvoll.

Claus kann nicht nein sagen und ist deshalb leider viel zu häufig mit Arbeit überlastet – trotzdem findet er erstaunlicherweise immer noch Zeit für sich selbst, seine Freunde und seine Ideen.

Diese Widersprüche scheinen bei Claus gut zu passen. Anders als bei den meisten talentierten und erfolgreichen Menschen gibt es nicht diese schwarze Wolke, die sich unerklärlich und unerwartet herabsenkt und seine Stimmung verschlingt.

Zeitweise scheint er die Zusammenhanglosigkeit seiner Welt und seines vielseitigen Charakters offen zu genießen.

Er scheint sogar eine Stütze darin zu finden.

Bei Claus haben wir es nicht mit einem leidenden, sondern mit einem glücklichen Künstler zu tun, der durch seine Misere eher angeregt wird.

Weil es ihm gelingt, die bösen Geister seiner eigenen Welt zu bändigen, ist er vielleicht auch fähig, die Schlacken professioneller Photographie abzustreifen und festzuhalten an seiner Ehrlichkeit, seiner Reinheit und Poesie.

Träume weiter, Claus.

David Colby

Personnellement, je pense que l'intelligence de Socrate était supérieure à celle de Newton, je fais donc un compliment à Claus lorsque je dis qu'il possède, lui aussi, cette qualité peu commune, la logique intuitive.

Il serait tentant d'affirmer que sa pensée n'est pas guidée par sa tête mais par son cœur, néanmoins, c'est faux.

Claus est trop contradictoire pour cela.

Bien qu'il soit un rêveur invétéré, il est capable de se concentrer intensément. C'est l'un des plus grands travailleurs que j'aie jamais rencontrés.

Il mène une vie extravagante, mais sa prodigalité lui importe peu.

On a toujours le sentiment que quand Claus quittera la pièce, ce sera pour aller s'acheter un sac à dos ultramoderne horriblement cher et s'éclipser.

Au fond, il est naïf mais, comme chez la plupart des artistes, cela donne justement un style recherché à son travail.

Claus ne sait pas dire non et est malheureusement souvent surchargé de travail. Toutefois, et c'est étonnant, il trouve encore du temps pour lui-même, ses amis et ses idées.

Ses contradictions lui vont bien.

Il n'est pas semblable à la plupart des individus talentueux qui ont réussi. Aucun nuage sombre ne tombe sans crier gare pour troubler sa bonne humeur.

On dirait parfois qu'il savoure les contradictions de son monde et de son caractère. Il semble même y trouver un soutien.

Avec Claus, nous n'avons pas affaire à un artiste souffrant, mais à un artiste heureux, motivé par sa condition.

C'est peut-être parce qu'il parvient à apprivoiser les démons de son propre monde qu'il est aussi capable de se frayer un chemin dans la jungle de la photographie professionnelle tout en restant un poète honnête et pur.

Continue de rêver, Claus.

David Colby

Flowerskin.

My whole life long I've lived with flowers.
I've collected and dried them.
I keep them as bookmarks in all my books.
I see them everywhere.
These photographs express the simple idea of images without
accessories, special backgrounds or tricky light effects.
The connection of Nature and Human Being.
I've tried to be as honest as possible to find out
visually how close I feel and live with Nature,
to forget the duality in which we are all living,
and to understand beauty in its simplicity.
Only then can we truly understand a flower.
Just as a flower lives, having no past without any future,
living and dying for the beauty of the moment.
Flowers never die.

Blumen begleiten mich durch mein ganzes Leben.
Ich habe sie gesammelt und getrocknet.
Als Lesezeichen finden sie sich in allen meinen Büchern.
Ich sehe sie überall.
Diese Aufnahmen zeigen ganz einfach Bilder ohne Zubehör, ohne
spezielle Hintergründe oder komplizierte Lichteffekte.
Die Verbindung von Natur und Mensch.
Ich habe versucht, so aufrichtig wie möglich zu sein, um
visuell herauszufinden, wie stark ich mich mit der Natur verbunden fühle,
um zu vergessen was für ein zweiseitiges Dasein wir führen,
und um die Schönheit in ihrer einfachsten Form zu ergründen.
Nur so können wir das Wesen einer Blume wirklich verstehen.
Verstehen, wie sie lebt, und begreifen, daß sie
keine Vergangenheit und keine Zukunft hat,
sondern für einen Moment der Schönheit lebt und stirbt.
Blumen vergehen niemals.

Toute ma vie durant, j'ai vécu entouré de fleurs.
Je les ai cueillies, je les ai fait sécher.
Je les garde comme marque-pages dans tous mes livres.
Elles sont partout autour de moi.
Ces photos expriment l'idée simple d'images sans accessoires,
arrière-plans bizarres cu éclairages clichés.
La Connexion entre la Nature et l'Etre humain.
J'ai essayé d'être le plus honnête possible afin
de trouver un langage visuel qui traduise à quel
point je suis en phase avec la Nature, dans le but
de me soustraire à la Dualité qui nous entoure et
de comprendre la Beauté dans son expression la plus
simple. Ce n'est seulement qu'après qu'il nous est vraiment
possible de comprendre ce qu'est une fleur.
Comment au juste une fleur vit, sans passé et sans aucun futur,
vivant et mourant pour la Beauté de l'instant.
Les fleurs ne meurent jamais.

Claus Wickrath

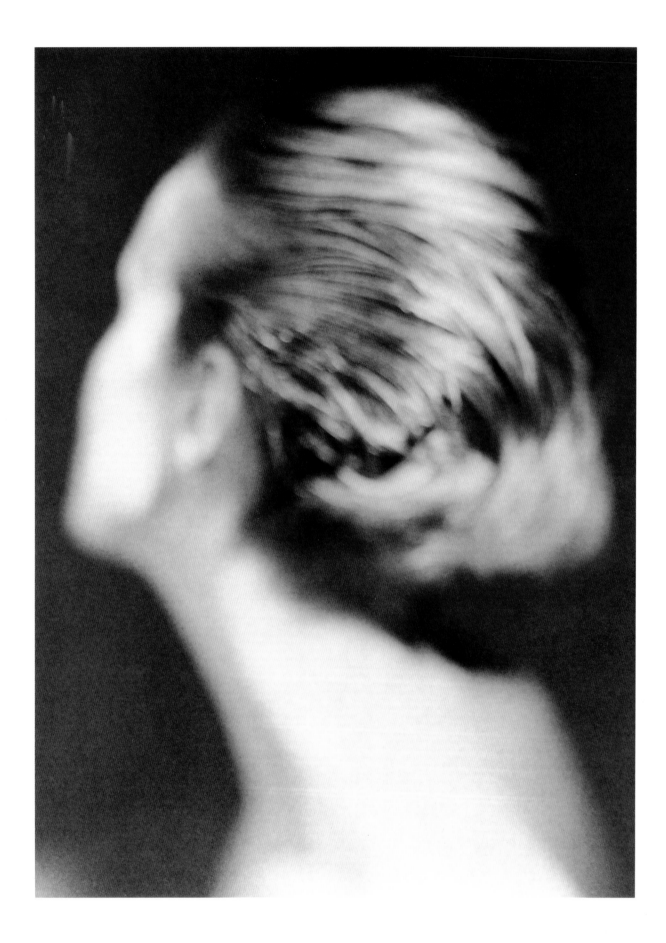

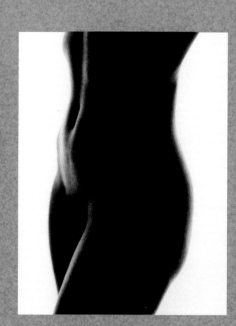

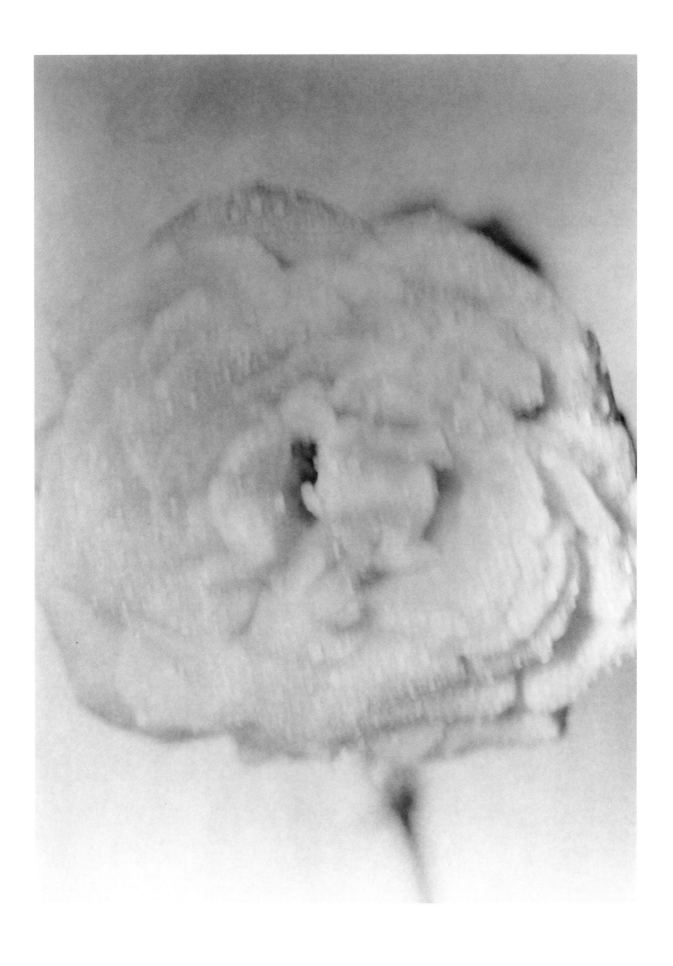

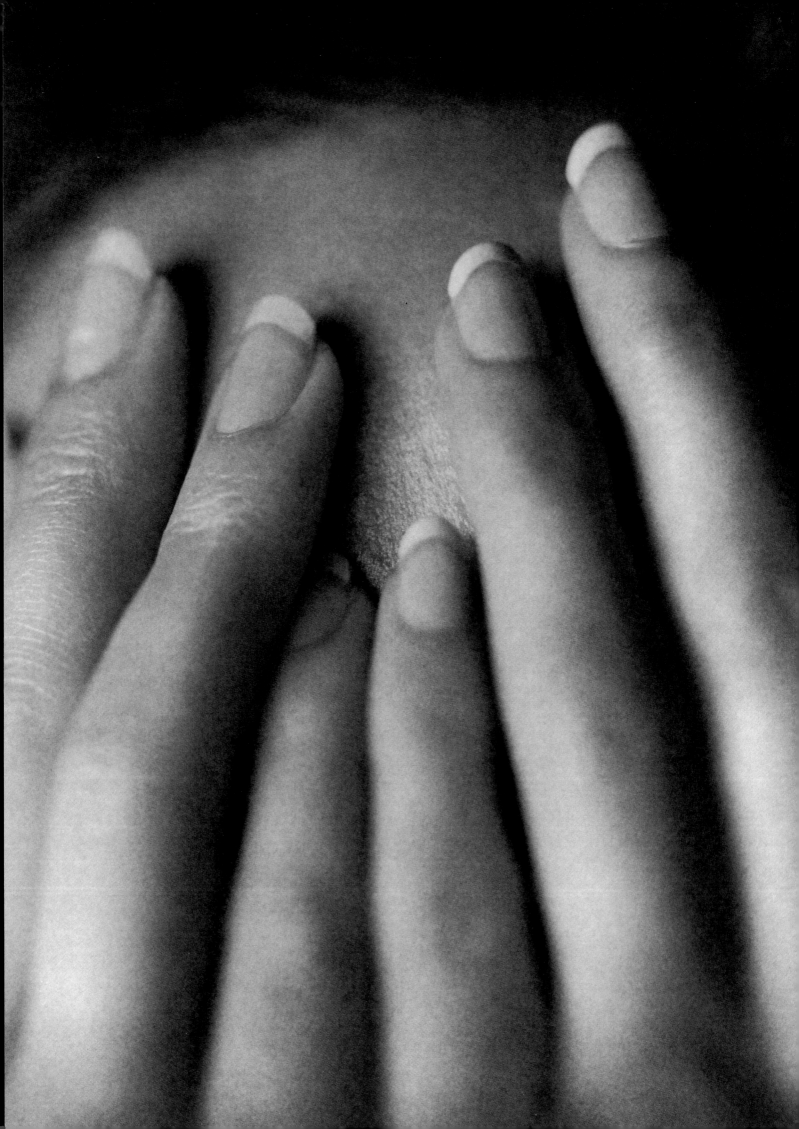

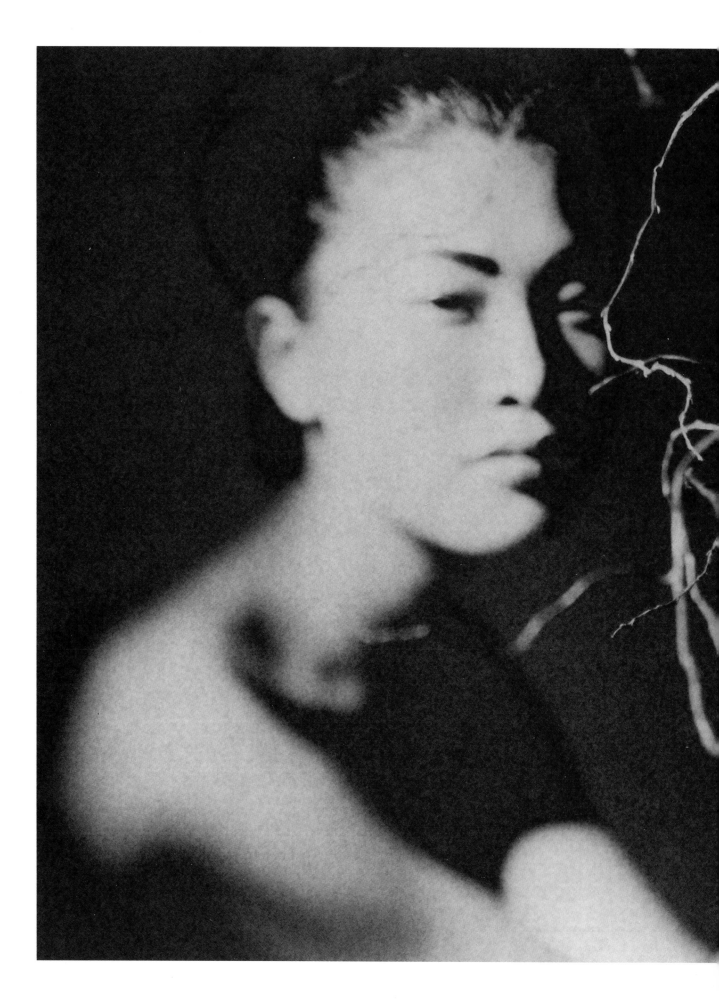

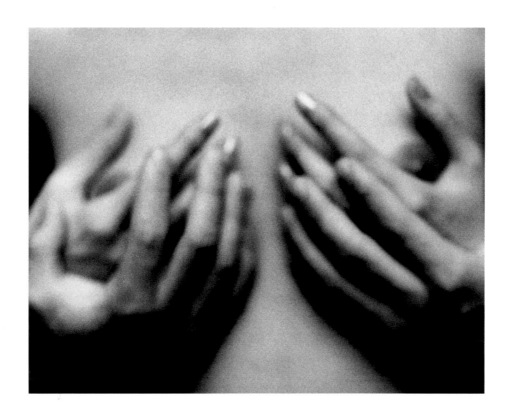

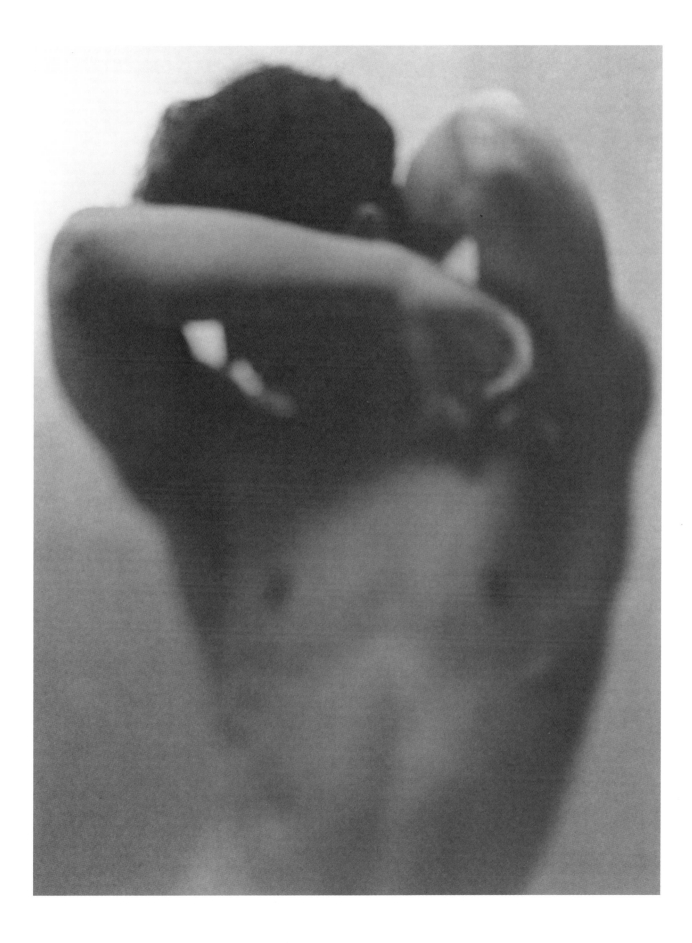

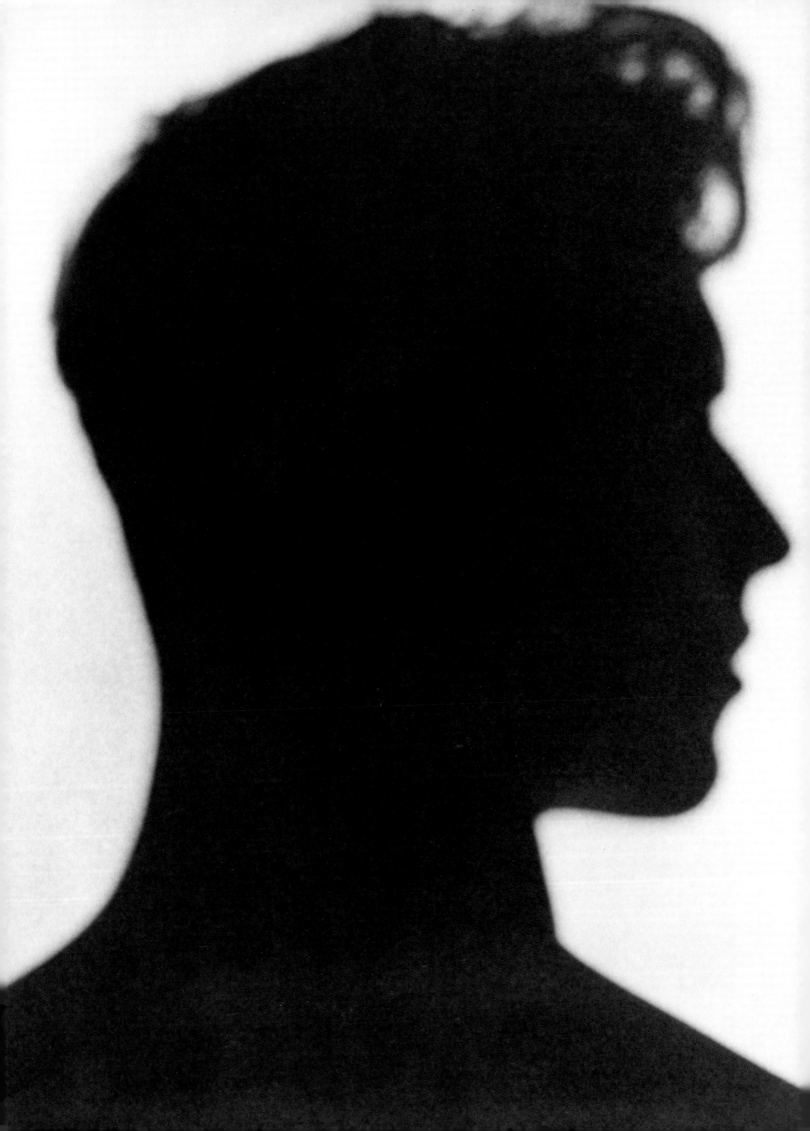

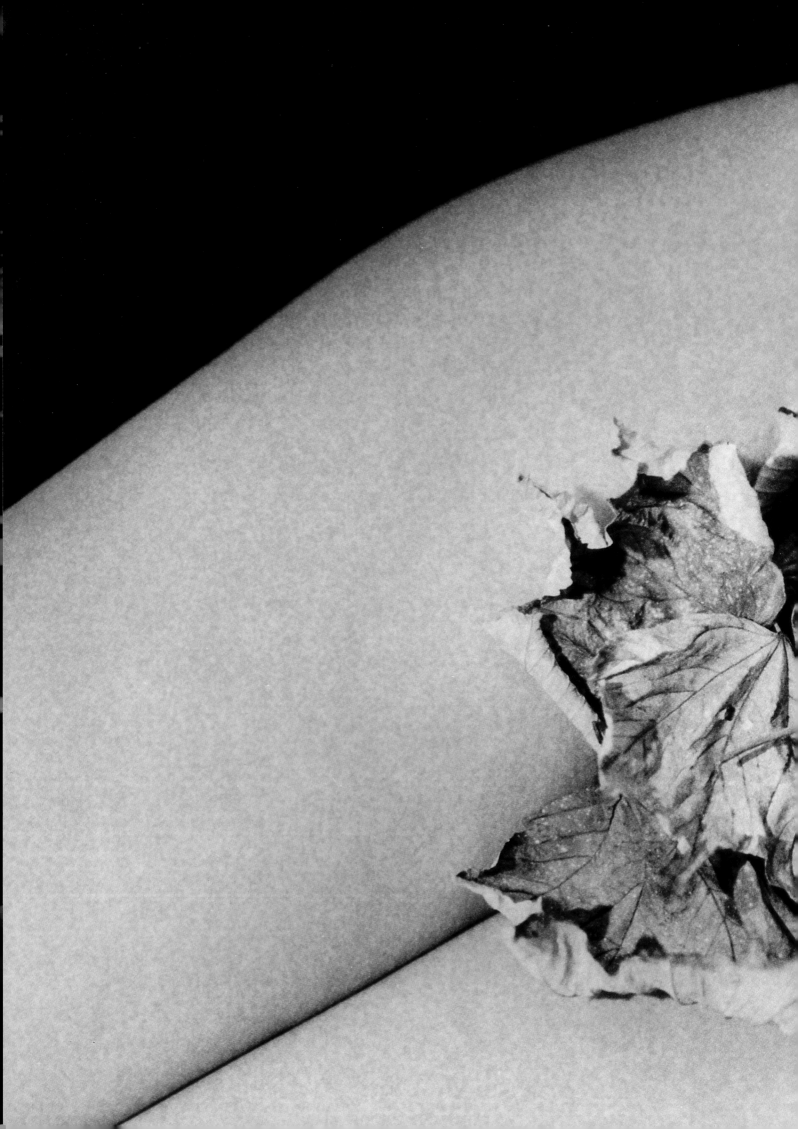

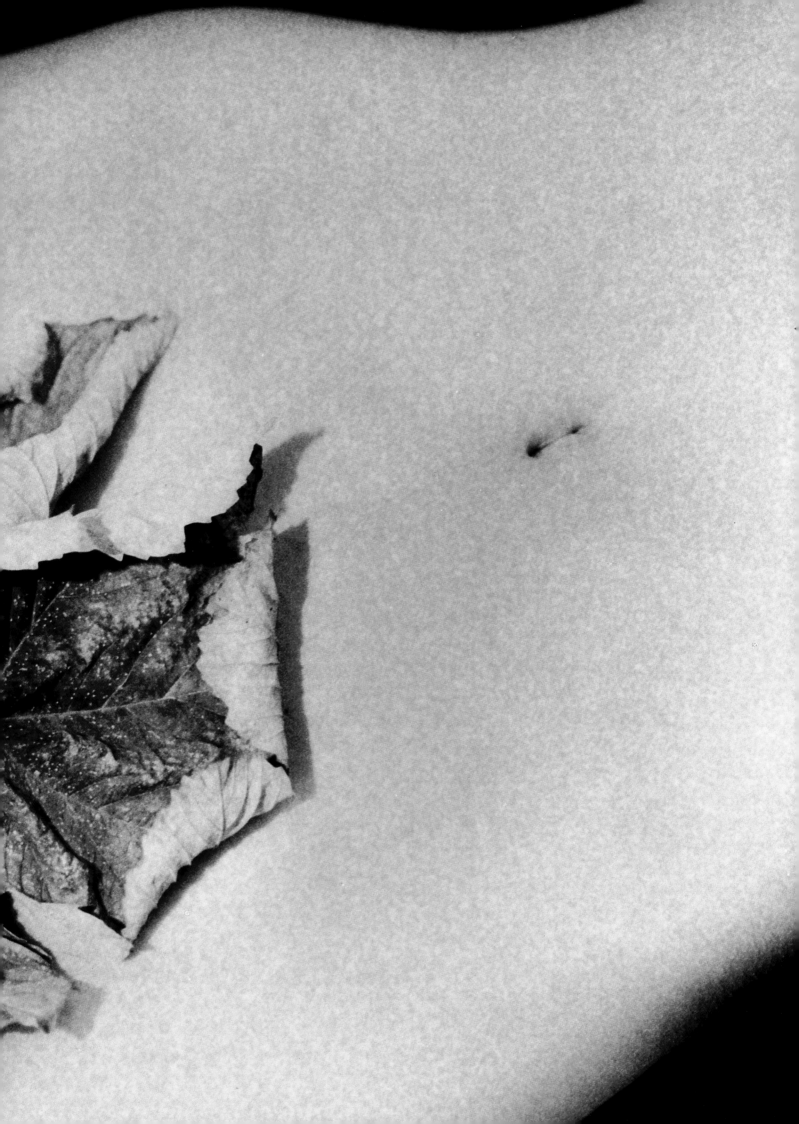

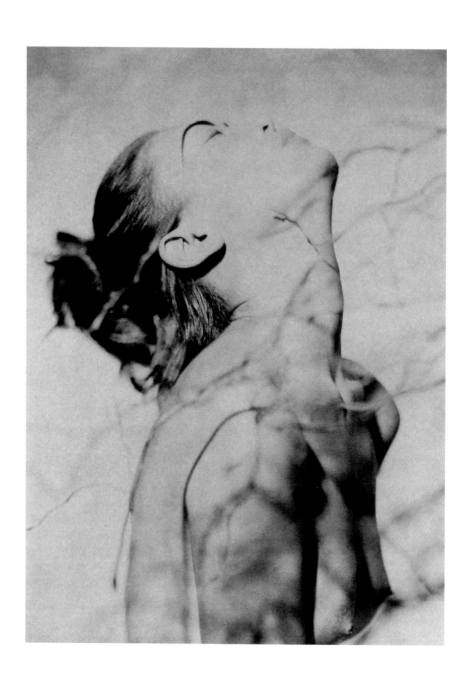

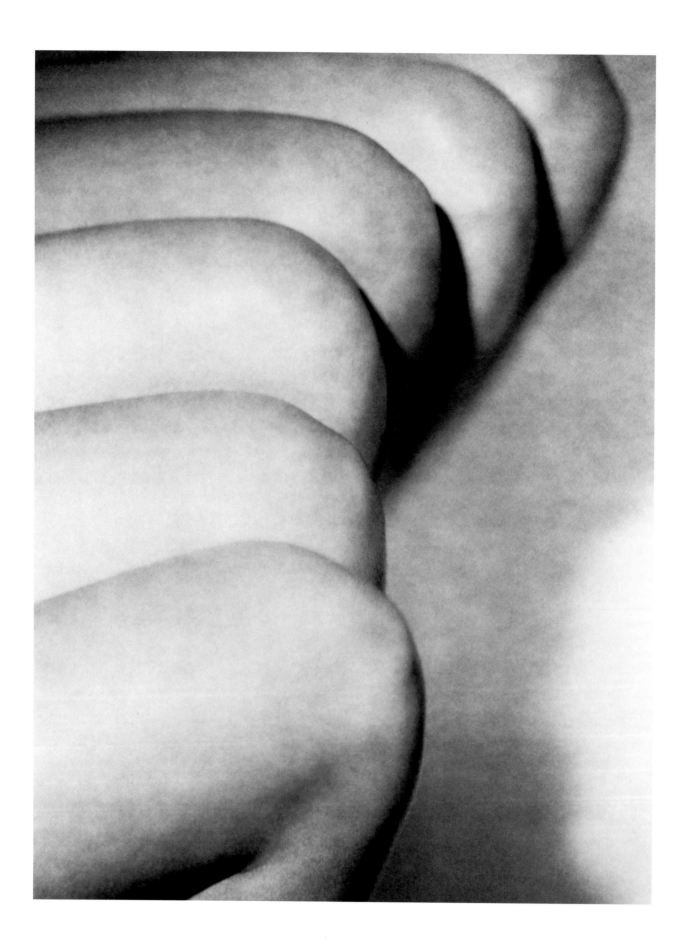

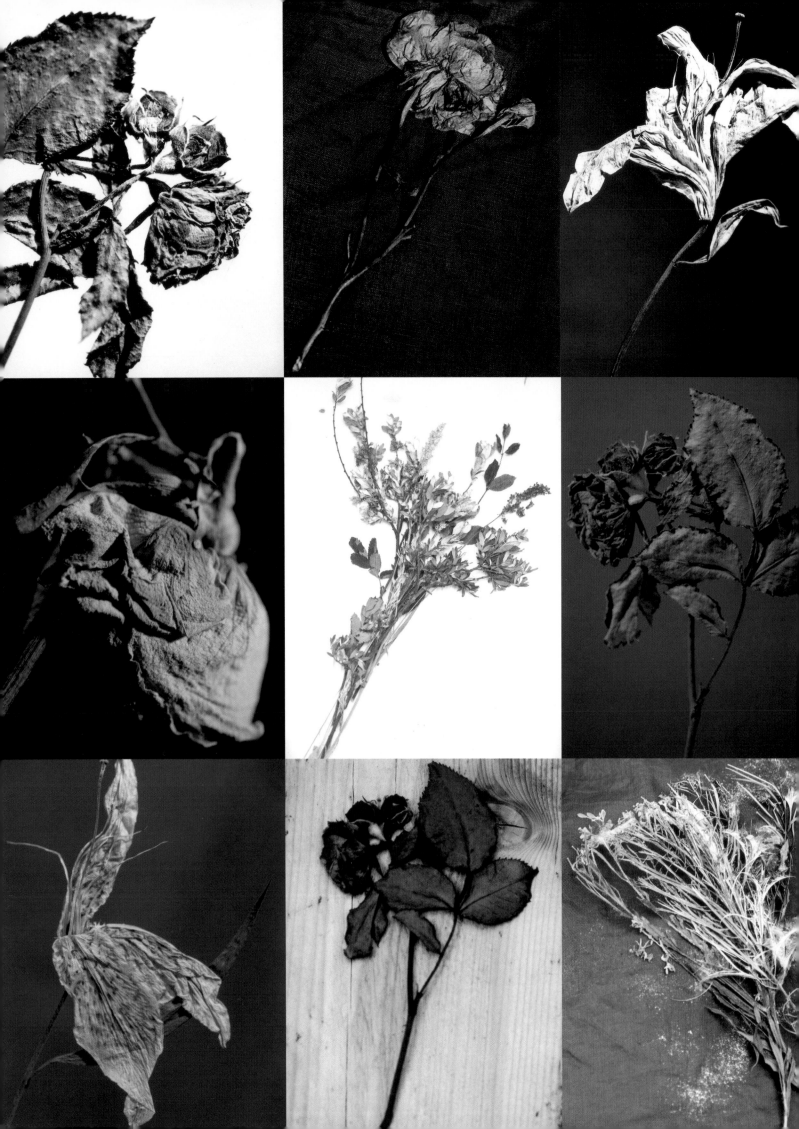

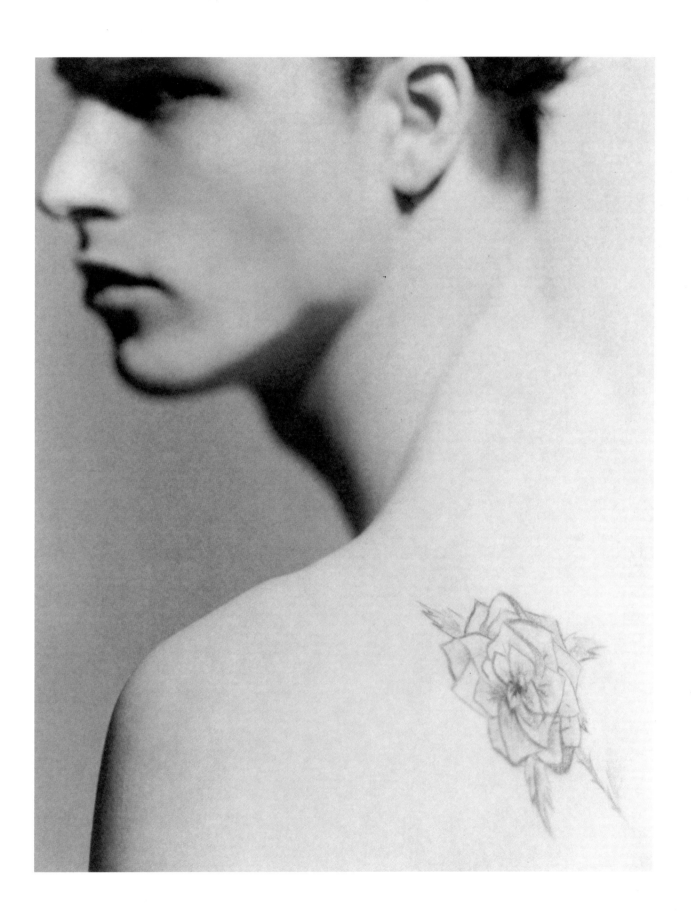

Thank you very much
Monica, Will, Laetitia,
Wel Mei, Jaimie, Nieves,
Dominique, Andrea, Nick,
Ikeda, Nynne, Nathalie,
Susan, Giselle, Mariano,
Amina, Ricardo, Natalia.

Art Direction Yves Sabba

Make-up Topolino
Hair Makoto
Prints Black White
Organization Casting
Sabine Bolzen

Biography

Claus Wickrath born in Düsseldorf, Germany. Spends a happy childhood on his grandfather's farm.
Early interest in painting and music.
Aged seventeen, he forms his first band, playing blues and rock-and-roll and touring all over Germany and Holland.
His interest in music takes him to London for the first time.
In London he works for two years as assistant to the photographer John Vaughan.
As John is working for German clients, Claus returns to Germany. He decides to stay in Düsseldorf where he joins *Partners Studios* as an assistant.

1975   Sets up his own studio in Düsseldorf. First work for the advertising agency *Team/BBDO*.

1977   First editorial work in Hamburg for the magazines *Für Sie* and *Petra*.

1978   First jobs for *Petra* in *Clic-Clac Studios*, carried out in Paris due to the availability of models, hairdressers, props, locations. Decides to stay in Paris.

1979   First cover for the French magazine *Elle*.

1980   Receives an increasing number of commissions from Italy.

1982   First exhibition of photographs in Paris called *Hakalaht* (Above the clouds).

1984   Founds *Studio Kicks* in Paris.

1985   His daughter Zoë is born. Works on a book called *Hungry Years*.

1986   Travels the world for international magazines and advertising agencies.

1989   Works on a book in Colombia entitled *Momo*.

1990   *Flowerskin* is published.

Biographie

Claus Wickrath ist in Düsseldorf geboren. Verlebt eine harmonische Kindheit auf dem Hof seines Großvaters.
Frühes Interesse an Kunst und Musik. Mit 17 Jahren erste Tournee durch Deutschland und Holland mit einer eigenen Rockband.
Erste Reise nach London aus Interesse an Rockmusik.
Zweijähriger Aufenthalt in London als Assistent bei dem Fotografen John Vaughan.
Zusammen mit John Vaughan Rückkehr nach Deutschland, um für deutsche Kunden zu arbeiten.
Entscheidet sich, in Düsseldorf zu bleiben, und arbeitet für *Partners Studios* als Assistent.

1975   Erstes eigenes Studio in Düsseldorf. Erstes Engagement für die Werbeagentur *Team/BBDO*.

1977   Erste Arbeiten in Hamburg für die Magazine *Für Sie* und *Petra*.

1978   Organisiert erste Arbeiten für *Petra* in den *Clic-Clac Studios* in Paris wegen des leichteren Zugangs zu Modellen, Hair-Stylisten, Ausstattern und Locations.

1979   Erstes Cover für das französische Magazin *Elle*.

1980   Arbeitet zunehmend für italienische Auftraggeber.

1982   Erste Fotoausstellung in Paris, genannt *Hakalaht* (über den Wolken).

1984   Ruft *Studio Kicks* in Paris ins Leben.

1985   Geburt seiner Tochter Zoë. Arbeitet am Buch *Hungry Years*.

1986   Rund um die Welt unterwegs für internationale Magazine und Werbeagenturen.

1989   Aufenthalt in Kolumbien für das Buch *Momo*.

1990   Erscheint *Flowerskin*.

Biographie

Claus Wickrath est né à Düsseldorf, en Allemagne. Il passe une enfance heureuse à la ferme de son grand-père.
Il s'intéresse très tôt à la peinture et à la musique. A 17 ans, il forme un groupe de rock et fait sa première tournée en Allemagne et aux Pays-Bas. Il fait son premier voyage à Londres par amour du rock. Là, il travaille pendant deux ans en tant qu'assistant du photographe John Vaughan.
John devant travailler pour des clients allemands, il revient en Allemagne. Il décide de rester à Düsseldorf et de travailler en tant qu'assistant pour *Partners Studios*.

1975   Il ouvre son propre studio à Düsseldorf. Premier engagement pour l'agence de publicité *Team/BBDO*.

1977   Premiers travaux réalisés à Hambourg pour les magazines *Für Sie* et *Petra*.

1978   Premières photos pour *Petra*, réalisées aux *Studios Clic-Clac* à Paris. Il s'installe à Paris, où les mannequins, accessoiristes et locations en tout genre sont aisément disponibles.

1979   Première couverture pour la revue française Elle.

1980   Travaille de plus en plus pour des clients italiens.

1982   Première exposition à Paris. Elle s'intitule *Hakalaht* (Au-dessus des nuages).

1984   Il crée le *Studio Kicks* à Paris.

1985   Naissance de sa fille Zoë. Il prépare un livre intitulé *Hungry Years*.

1986   Il parcourt le monde entier pour des magazines internationaux et des agences de publicité.

1989   Il réalise le livre *Momo* en Colombie.

1990   Parution de *Flowerskin*.